The Beautiful Poetry of
Donald Trump

The Beautiful Poetry of
Donald Trump

Created by Rob Sears

CANONGATE

This edition published in Great Britain,
the USA and Canada in 2019 by Canongate Books Ltd

First published in Great Britain in 2017 by Canongate Books Ltd,
14 High Street, Edinburgh EH1 1TE

Distributed in the USA by Publishers Group West
and in Canada by Publishers Group Canada

canongate.co.uk

4

British Library Cataloguing-in-Publication Data
A catalogue record for this book is available on
request from the British Library

ISBN 978 1 78689 472 4

Cover concept by Rob Sears
Initial page design by Paula Amaral

Typeset in Minion Pro by Palimpsest Book Production Ltd,
Falkirk, Stirlingshire

Printed and bound in Great Britain by Clays Ltd, Elcograf S.p.A.

1 Inaugural address in Washington, DC, as the 45th President of the United States, 20 January 2017

People of the world,
thank you[1]

Editor's notes

It is a little known alternative fact that the 45th President, Donald J. Trump, has long been a remarkable poet. This book aims to redress this oversight on the part of the literary world, and showcase his finest and most revealing words in a previously unseen form. Whether discoursing on politics, walls, gender issues or his own excellent genes, Trump's poems are nothing if not beautiful. Terrific, in fact. Amazing. And they reveal a sensitive and shyly artistic side to Trump that may prompt a reappraisal of the man even among his critics.

One of the many charges levelled at Donald Trump by those in the fake news media is that his use of English is lazily repetitive, perhaps indicating a dunderheaded and unimaginative thinker. But consider works like 'My two favorite words' (p. 117). Repetitious yes, but to deliberate, mesmerising effect. And look at the words that he most often comes back to: 'love' twelve times in 'Everybody loves me' (p. 45); 'beautiful' twelve times in 'A beautiful, simple life' (p. 3). This is not the work of a monotonous man, but an aesthete for whom love and beauty are wells of feeling to return to and draw from.

There is a rebuttal here too to the charge that Trump's rambling public speaking style evidences a disordered brain. 'Slowly the hair dries', 'I am open-minded', 'Get ready for some excitement' and 'Fake news, folks' (pp. 53, 55, 95 and 61) display the precision and concentrated brevity of a modern-day Basho or Larkin. Then there are the Trump Haikus ('Little Marco', 'Sad sack Rosie', 'Lyin' Ted', 'Crazy Megyn Kelly', 'Crooked Hillary', 'Low energy Jeb', 'Deviant Anthony Weiner', 'Dopey Lord Sugar', 'Barack Hussein Obama (aka Barry Soetoro)', 'Wacko Glenn Beck', 'President Putin', 'Failing comedian Bill Maher', 'Goofy Elizabeth Warren' and 'Very foul-mouthed Sen. John McCain' – pp. 49, 81, 47, 75, 25, 99, 13, 39, 9, 63, 33, 109, 43 and 93). All are in formal 5-7-5 meter. All hit their targets like laser-guided Paveway missiles – testimony to a writer of supreme discipline and power.

On a superficial reading of some of the poems, critics may hear only the voice of the Trump they *think* they know. 'Photographic memory', 'I have the best words', 'Good genes', 'I'm really rich', 'Bad Hombres' and 'I am the most fabulous whiner' (pp. 87, 111, 91, 5, 31 and 17) are bracingly braggadocious. Others are elemental in their anger, as though he woke at 4 a.m. in a white-hot rage to gouge them into Mar-a-Lago letterpaper (see 'These people are losers', 'This country is going to hell in a handbasket', 'Pervert alert', 'Does torture work?', 'Get the oil, get the oil, get the oil', 'No days off' and 'We've got to stop the stupid' (pp. 37, 7, 77, 59, 69, 83 and 65). But there is more here than technique and combative spirit. If we allow ourselves to listen, we can also hear the counterpoint of a quieter, less self-assured Trump, as when he breaks off his list of boasts in 'I am the best' (p. 23) to worry about the size of his appendages.

Trump fully exposes his vulnerable underbelly in the poems 'I want to be good', 'What's going on? What's going on?', and the ironic 'I won!' (pp. 101, 119 and 19). Here we get a glimpse of real tragedy – a man born to win coming to terms with his awareness of his own failings – and it is hard to come away unmoved. Yet he never succumbs to self-obsession. In 'All I ask is fairness', 'Very dishonest media', 'My hands are normal hands', 'Look at the way I've been treated lately' and 'I am the least racist person there is' (pp. 35, 57, 103, 115 and 11), it is the injustice of a broken system and the effect of biased journalism on his country that drives Trump to verse.

'A dream', 'I love to read' and 'I don't know' (pp. 113, 107 and 121) explore the innermost and least mapped parts of Trump's psyche. 'I am the innocent (pure) one!' (p. 97) marks a foray into metaphysical poetry; in effect, it is a love letter to the entire universe. Although Melania Trump is, interestingly, not mentioned in any of the poems, we can also see Trump's more traditional romantic persona rising to the fore in poems such as 'Hot little girl in high school' (p. 67), and 'Look at this baby' (p. 51) while two further poems comment wryly on the issue of gender relations, something Trump perhaps understands better than he lets on ('I respect women, I love women, I cherish women' and 'Women have one of the great acts of all time' – pp. 41 and 79).

The greatest misapprehension about DJT corrected by this volume, however, may be the idea that he sees money and power as ends in themselves. In fact, just as Wilfred Owen turned his wartime experience into poetry, and Sylvia Plath found the dark beauty in her own depression, Trump is able to transform his unique experiences of being a winner into 24-karat verse. He didn't build a huge real-estate empire for the billions; he did it so he could write poems like 'Treat yourself to the very, very best life has to offer' and 'We are going to have to get rid of them' (pp. 71 and 27). He didn't go to Washington to be feared; he did it so he could alchemise his experiences into the poems 'MAGA!', 'There's something going on that we don't know about', 'I make this promise', 'You can do anything' and 'We have by far the highest IQ of any Cabinet ever assembled' (pp. 15, 85, 21, 73 and 29). And for his verse, he is prepared to risk everything – quite literally, the Earth (see 'We'll be fine with the environment' and 'Pittsburgh, not Paris' – pp. 89 and 105).

For readers who have trouble enjoying Trump's poems because of their pre-existing views of his politics, one poem in particular, the Whitmanesque 'You have to be everything' (p. 123), is key. Here Trump advances a sophisticated theory of identity. He posits that we each contain many overlapping selves, each enacting different, sometimes contradictory performative roles. This helps us see how Trump the President can coexist with Trump the CEO, Trump the TV Mogul, Trump the Family Man – and Trump the Poet. You do not have to accept one to appreciate the other.

N.B. To ensure the poems' clarity of meaning, the Editor has changed references to people's Twitter handles to their names, eliminated hashtags, has on occasion reduced words in all capitals to lower case, and, where aesthetically appropriate, removed the occasional exclamation point and changed ampersands to 'and'.

Rob Sears, 2017

Postscript to the editor's notes (second edition)

Admirers of Donald Trump's poetry may be worried that the continuing demands of the presidency have weakened his artistic vigour. Thankfully the opposite is true. Since the first edition of this book was published, Trump has produced some of his most mature poems yet, seventeen of which are included in this edition.

Where a lesser artist would be drained by the twenty-hour days and stresses of high office, Trump (perhaps the healthiest individual ever to attempt an ABAB rhyming scheme) is inspired and invigorated.

Take the three-poem NoKo sequence, which charts the easing of tensions between Trump and Kim Jong-un in 2018 ('Everyone does get a little nervous when I press that button', 'Little "Rocket Man"' and 'The gift of friendship', pp. 127, 129 and 131). Even aside from their historical import, these are poems that will be studied in years to come for their touching treatment of a blossoming friendship.

As his first term continues to unfold, each new political episode provides Trump with the high emotions on which his poetry thrives, whether he's on cloud nine after a successful arms deal ('Art of the deal', and 'Very big negotiations', pp. 125

and 141); stewing over the FBI collusion probe ('NO COLLUSION (Except by the Dems)!', 'Slippery James Comey, the worst FBI director in history: a Haiku', and 'Achomlishments', pp. 145, 147 and 157); or celebrating the diversity of his nation ('Shithole countries' and 'Aliens', pp. 133 and 137).

A cynic might accuse Trump of drama-chasing his way through his first term to fuel his real concern – his poetic practice. But trace some of his most intense emotions, recollected in tranquility in new poems such as 'How totally stupid is this guy?', 'I don't think Angelina Jolie is good looking' and 'The mighty oceans' (pp. 135, 139 and 143) and it's clear that he can turn pretty much anything into beautiful poetry, from his opinions on Isaac Newton to his hatred of sharks.

Only an artist as driven as Trump could maintain this level of consistent output and quality with so many other demands on his attention. One pictures him awake, alone in the small hours of Christmas Eve in the tinsel-festooned Oval Office bedroom, overcome by festive compulsion to scribble down 'The Christmas of Trump' and 'What's with the get-up, Kringle?' (pp. 151 and 153). Or waking in a chilly sweat in his hotel suite at the G8 Summit in Quebec to transcribe from his subconscious the haunting future classic, 'A nightmare' (p. 149); or pausing Fox's late-night analysis of the Supreme Court confirmation hearings to meditate on the rosy red face of his judicial hero, in 'Perfect human being Brett Kavanaugh: a Haiku' (p. 155).

In the light of these new works, it bears repeating: whatever we think of his politics, we can surely all agree that Trump's dedication to the art of poetry, at least, remains unimpeachable.

The Poems

1 *Happening Now*, 12 October 2016
2 *With All Due Respect*, MSNBC, 29 March 2016
3 Remarks from the USS *Gerald R. Ford* in Virginia, 17 December 2016
4 Remarks at the Congressional Republican Retreat in Philadelphia, 26 January 2017
5 *Anderson Cooper 360*, CNN, 5 July 2016
6 Campaign rally in Muscatine, Iowa, CSPAN, 25 January 2016
7 Tweet promoting Miss Universe Pageant, 7 December 2012
8 Key Capitol Hill hearings, CSPAN, 27 February 2015
9 *The O'Reilly Factor*, Fox News, 28 April 2016
10 National Press Club luncheon, CSPAN, 31 May 2014
11 *Hannity*, Fox News, 15 July 2015
12 *Hannity*, Fox News, 15 August 2015
13 Hotel opening, CSPAN, 27 October 2016

A beautiful, simple life[1]

Beautiful bikes[2]
Beautiful aircraft carriers[3]
Beautiful coal[4]
Beautiful lie by Crooked Hillary[5]
Beautiful hats[6]
Beautiful women[7]
Beautiful tanks[8]
Beautiful Humvees[9]
Beautiful copper piping[10]
Beautiful auto plant[11]
Beautiful marines[12]
I've never seen scissors that look this beautiful before[13]

I'm really rich[1]

I'm very proud of my new crystal collection[2]
I have a Gucci store that's worth more than Romney[3]
I order thousands of televisions a year[4]
Six people do nothing but sort my mail[5]
Sorry haters and losers![6]
He who has the gold makes the rules[7]

This country is going to hell in a handbasket[1]

It just seems that our country is not what it used to be[2]

New York Fashion Week is really bad and used to be so glamorous and exciting[3]

Vanity Fair Magazine, which used to be one of my favorites, is failing badly[4]

A lot of people are switching to these really long putters. Very unattractive[5]

Our poor, poor country[6]

Barack Hussein Obama
(aka Barry Soetoro):[1] a Haiku

Is not who you think[2]
The worst ever President[3]
Founder of ISIS[4]

1 *Fox & Friends*, Fox News, 9 May 2011
2 Interview on Talk1300 AM, 14 April 2011
3 Tweet referencing Tiger Woods' marital infidelity and later victory at Trump National Doral, 20 March 2013
4 In answer to a question about possible VP picks in an interview with Larry King, 7 October 1999
5 Press conference, 3 September 2015
6, 7 *Playboy* interview, 1 October 2004
8 Annotation by Trump on article by Jonathan Capehart, which he sent to the journalist – tweeted by Capehart, 8 July 2015

I am the least racist person there is[1]

I've always had a great relationship with the blacks[2]

I remained strong for Tiger Woods during his difficult period[3]

Oprah, I love Oprah. Oprah would always be my first choice[4]

Kanye West – I love him[5]

I think Eminem is fantastic, and most people think I wouldn't like Eminem[6]

And did you know my name is in more black songs than any other name in hip-hop?[7]

You are the racist, not I[8]

Deviant Anthony Weiner:[1] a Haiku

Very sick puppy[2]
A screamer and a shouter[3]
He will never change[4]

1 Tweet criticising Hillary Clinton, 21 December 2015
2 Tweet referencing Will Smith's red carpet incident,
   21 May 2012
3 Campaign rally in St Augustine, Florida, 24 October 2016
4 Tweet criticising Sarah Jessica Parker, 26 October 2012
5 Tweet, 3 February 2017
6 Discussing female beauty in an interview on *The Howard Stern Show*, 2005
7 *Hardball with Chris Matthews*, MSNBC, 22 April 2016

MAGA!¹

Will Smith did a great job by smacking the guy "reporter"
who kissed him[2]
Together we're going to fix our rigged system[3]
Sarah Jessica Parker voted "unsexiest woman alive"
– I agree[4]
We must keep "evil" out of our country[5]
A person who is very flat chested is very hard to be
a ten[6]
We're going to make America great again[7]

1, 3, 5, 6, 7, 9, 10 *New Day*, CNN, 11 August 2015
2 Trump town hall, CNN, 12 April 2016
4 CNN Special, 3 March 2016
8 Campaign stop at Albemarle Estates, Virginia, 14 July 2015

I am the most fabulous whiner[1]

I own the largest winery on the east coast[2]
I do whine[3]
We make the finest wine[4]
Because I want to win[5]
And I'm not happy about not winning[6]
And I am a whiner[7]
Many different kind of wines[8]
And I'm a whiner and I keep whining and whining until I win[9]
And I'm going to win[10]

1 Tweet referencing US Presidential debate, 21 October 2016
2 *The Apprentice*, 2004 season

I won![1]

Well, we've had some disasters, but this is the worst[2]

1 Republican nomination acceptance speech, 21 July 2016
2 Presidential inauguration vows, 20 January 2017
3 Presidential bid announcement at Trump Tower, 16 June 2015, referring to a leg injury sustained by then Secretary of State John Kerry
4 *Larry King Live,* 8 October 1999
5 Tweet directed at Cher, 13 November 2012
6 Speech in Hilton Head, South Carolina, 30 December 2015

I make this promise[1]

I, Donald John Trump, do solemnly swear that I will faithfully execute the Office of President of the United States, and will to the best of my ability, preserve, protect and defend the Constitution of the United States[2]

I promise I will never be in a bicycle race[3]

I will not rename the White House[4]

And I promise not to talk about your massive plastic surgeries that didn't work[5]

I promise. Thank you[6]

1 Tweet, 8 August 2013
2 Tweet referencing Apple, Inc. stock price drop, 28 January 2014
3 Presidential bid announcement at Trump Tower, 16 June 2015
4 Campaign rally in Plymouth, New Hampshire, CSPAN,
   7 February 2016
5 *Hannity*, Fox News, 29 February 2016

I am the best[1]

I predicted Apple's stock fall[2]
I will build a great, great wall[3]
I build buildings that are 94 storeys tall[4]
My hands aren't – are they small?[5]

Crooked Hillary:[1] a Haiku

She got schlonged, she lost[2]
A nasty horrid woman[3]
Time to drain the swamp[4]

1 Referring to ISIS in an interview with Circa, 7 August 2016
2 Tweet criticising Anthony Weiner, 6 July 2012
3 Interview answer with Sean Hannity about ISIS fighters, 26 January 2017
4 Interview with *The New York Times*, 23 November 2016
5 Speech in Washington DC, 27 April 2016
6 Tweet referencing Trump Tower restaurant, Trump Grill, 29 November 2012

We are going to have to get rid of them[1]

Weasels are hard to get rid of[2]

They don't wear uniforms. They're sneaky, dirty rats[3]

It's been 18 months of brutality in a true sense[4]

But we won[5]

Trump Grill just received the highest sanitary inspection grade possible[6]

We have by far the highest IQ of any Cabinet ever assembled[1]

I appointed today the head secretary of the Veterans Administration, David Shulkin[2]

General Kelly is going to do a fantastic job at Homeland Security[3]

Ben Affleck is going to do a great job as Batman[4]

1 Presidential debate at the University of Nevada, Las Vegas, 19 October 2016
2 Live town hall event, *Today*, NBC, 21 April 2016
3 Live town hall event, *Today*, NBC, 21 April 2016
4 *Hannity*, Fox News, 27 August 2016
5 *Meet the Press*, MSNBC, 10 January 2016
6 Key Capitol Hill hearings, 30 December 2015
7 MSNBC, 12 March 2016
8 Tweet, 17 May 2013

Bad hombres[1]

I've known some bad dudes[2]
I've been at parties[3]
They want to do serious harm[4]
I've seen and I've watched things like with guns[5]
I know a lot of tough guys but they're not smart[6]
We're dealing with people that are animals[7]

But they are the folks I like the best – by far![8]

1 Tweet referencing Russian air strikes against ISIS, 16 November 2015
2 *Morning Joe*, MSNBC, 18 December 2015
3 Tweet claiming praise from Vladimir Putin, 27 July 2016
4 Receiving 'a great honor' of a compliment from 'a man so highly respected within his own country and beyond', at a rally in Columbus, Ohio, 17 December 2015

President Putin:[1] a Haiku

Is a strong leader[2]
Said "Trump is a genius"[3]
Highly respected[4]

1 After addressing the National Federation of Republican
   Assemblies in Nashville, Tennessee, 30 August 2015
2 *This Week*, ABC News, 19 July 2015
3 *Inside Politics*, CNN, 11 January 2017
4 Tweet criticising Barack Obama, 8 December 2013
5 Comment at rally in Albuquerque, New Mexico, 24 May 2016,
   in reference to Hillary Clinton loyalist Ed Rendell's statement
   about 'ugly women'

All I ask is fairness[1]

People are constantly attacking my hair[2]
I think it's very unfair[3]
Obama said he never met his uncle, Oscar[4]
Imagine if I made that statement?
It would be the electric chair[5]

1, 9 *Early Start with John Berman and Christine Romans*, CNN, 1
    June 2016
2   Tweet criticising Jeb Bush's Republican Presidential nominee
    campaign, 2 January 2016
3   *Entertainment Tonight*, CBS, 21 December 2006
4   Tweet criticising Carly Fiorina, 21 September 2015
5   Tweet criticising Sacha Baron Cohen, 27 February 2012
6   Tweet criticising Jon Stewart, 30 May 2015
7   *News 3 Live at Twelve-Thirty*, NBC, 25 August 2016
8   Tweet criticising Lord Alan Sugar's conflict with Piers Morgan,
    10 December 2012
10 Tweet criticising Lord Alan Sugar, 6 December 2012

These people are losers[1]

Jeb Bush is a low energy stiff[2]

Rosie O'Donnell's disgusting, both inside and out[3]

Carly Fiorina is terrible at business[4]

Sacha Baron Cohen is a moron[5]

Jon Stewart is a joke, not very bright and totally overrated[6]

Cher is somewhat of a loser[7]

Lord Sugar – you're a total loser who Piers Morgan doesn't think is very smart or very rich[8]

These people are losers[9]

Thank the real Lord that Donald Trump exists[10]

1 Tweet criticising Lord Alan Sugar, 6 December 2012
2 Tweet criticising Lord Alan Sugar, 10 May 2013
3 Tweet criticising Lord Alan Sugar, 11 May 2013
4 Tweet criticising Lord Alan Sugar, 7 December 2012

Dopey Lord Sugar:[1] a Haiku

Can't get himself arrested[2]
Is a laughing stock[3]
A total loser[4]

1 No Labels Problem Solver Convention in Manchester, New
   Hampshire, 12 October 2015
2 Howard Stern recounts comment made by Trump at the latter's
   wedding to Maria Maples, *The Howard Stern Show*, January 1997
3 Tweet supporting birther movement, 27 August 2012

I respect women, I love women, I cherish women[1]

Vagina is expensive[2]
No more apologies – take the offensive![3]

1 Tweet criticising Elizabeth Warren and Hillary Clinton's US
   Presidential campaign, 6 May 2016
2 Tweet insulting Elizabeth Warren, 10 June 2016
3 Phone call to NBC News derisively referencing Elizabeth
   Warren's Native American heritage, 27 July 2016
4 Tweet questioning Elizabeth Warren's Native American heritage,
   6 May 2016

Goofy Elizabeth Warren:[1] a Haiku

Has a nasty mouth[2]
We call her Pocahontas[3]
I say she's a fraud[4]

1　Interview with Anderson Cooper, CNN, 8 July 2015
2　Interview with Bob Woodward and Robert Costas, 8 April 2016
3　Address to supporters in Lawrenceville, New Jersey, CSPAN, 20 May 2016
4　Interview with CNN, 21 February 2016
5　*Washington This Week*, CSPAN, 3 April 2016
6　*CNN Tonight with Don Lemon*, CNN, 30 September 2015
7　*New York Magazine*, 13 December 2004
8　*Morning Joe*, MSNBC, 24 July 2015
9　*Media Buzz*, Fox News, 25 January 2016
10　*First Look*, MSNBC, 4 September 2015
11　*America This Morning*, ABC, 9 October 2015
12　*Meet the Press*, NBC, 24 January 2016
13　*Anderson Cooper 360 GOP Town Hall*, CNN, 19 February 2016
14　Remarks at Iowa State Fair on how he believed people would respond to his immigration policies, 15 August 2015
15　Tweet threatening Ted Cruz, 22 March 2016

Everybody loves me[1]

Tom Brady loves me[2]

The people of New York, they love me[3]

Upstate New York, I'm like the most popular person that's ever lived[4]

The bikers love me[5]

You know who loves me? The Tea Party, the evangelicals[6]

My children could not love me more if I spent fifteen times more time with them[7]

The vets love me[8]

The African Americans love me[9]

The Asians love me[10]

Many Hispanics who love me[11]

Most conservatives love me[12]

Society loves me[13]

You are going to love me[14]

Or I will spill the beans on your wife![15]

1 Tweet criticising Ted Cruz, 1 April 2016
2 Tweet criticising Ted Cruz, 25 January 2016
3 Tweet criticising Ted Cruz, 13 February 2016
4 Reference to audience member at rally, Manchester, New Hampshire, 9 February 2016

Lyin' Ted:[1] a Haiku

A nervous wreck[2]
Holds the bible high and then lies[3]
He's a pussy[4]

Little Marco:[1] a Haiku

Not presidential[2]
Like a little boy on stage[3]
Very short and lies[4]

1 Speech in Tampa, Florida, 5 November 2016
2 Speech in Loudon County, Virginia, 2 August 2016
3 Cutting short an interview on *Face the Nation*, CBS, 1 May 2017
4, 5 Discussing extending his family in an interview on *The Howard Stern Show*.
6 Commenting on the current Mexican border fences on *60 Minutes*, 27 September 2015

Look at this baby[1]

That is a great, beautiful baby[1]
It's young and beautiful and healthy[2]
I love babies[2]
What a baby[2]
What a beautiful baby[2]
...
Okay that's enough[3]
You can get the baby out of here[2]
I like kids[4]
I won't do anything to take care of them[5]
They're ugly, little and don't work[6]

1 *Playboy* interview, 2004
2 Conference call with members of the Alabama Republican Party, 11 September 2015

Slowly the hair dries[1]

It's a process that can take 18 months to two years[2]

1 *Fox News Sunday*, Fox News, 11 December 2016
2 Tweet criticising Apple, Inc. stance on encryption, 19 February 2016
3 Donald Trump (2016), *Great Again: How to Fix Our Crippled America*, Threshold Editions, Simon & Schuster: New York, p. 96

I am open-minded[1]

I use both iPhone and Samsung[2]
A great leader has to be flexible[3]

Very dishonest media[1]

The BBC is in total disarray[2]
The failing *New York Times* gets worse and worse by the day[3]
The leaks are absolutely real. The news is fake[4]
I'm turning to Fox News where we get a fair shake[5]
Watched *Saturday Night Live* hit job on me[6]
I don't call it thin-skinned. I'm angry[7]

1, 4 Interview on *ABC News*, ABC, 25 January 2017
2 Referring to plans to tax Chinese goods in speech in Las Vegas, 28 April 2011
3 Interview on *60 Minutes*, CBS, 27 September 2015
5 Tweet supporting use of sleep deprivation on terrorist suspects, 11 December 2014
6 Tweet with video link of Trump singing a cover version of Carly Rae Jepsen's 'Call Me Maybe' with Giuliana Rancic, 6 September 2012
7 Campaign rally in Denver, Colorado, 1 August 2016

Does torture work?[1]

Listen you motherfuckers[2]
Not everything is nice[3]
Waterboarding[4]
Sleep deprivation[5]
Me singing "Call me maybe"[6]
I'm not saying it's pleasant but believe me, it works[7]

1 Supporters' rally in Nashville, Tennessee, 15 March 2017
2 WWE Hall of Fame acceptance speech, 6 April 2013
3 News conference, 3 November 2015

Fake news, folks[1]

It all began with WrestleMania number 4[2]
That was staged by the Democrats[3]

Wacko Glenn Beck:[1] a Haiku

Crying lost soul[2]
Got fired like a dog by Fox[3]
Mental basketcase[4]

We've got to stop the stupid[1]

You know what uranium is, right?[2]

It's a thing called nuclear weapons and other things like lots of things that are done with uranium including some bad things[3]

I have to explain to these people, they don't understand basic physics, basic mathematics, whatever you want to call it[4]

I mean, they're like stupid[5]

1 Discussing losing his virginity on *The Howard Stern Show*, 1997
2 Tweet, 21 April 2013
3 Quoted as saying this to two fourteen-year-old girls in the *Chicago Tribune*, December 1992
4 To Brande Roderick on *The Celebrity Apprentice*, 2013 season
5 *The New Yorker*, 19 May 1997
6 Speech after winning Florida, Illinois and North Carolina primaries, 15 March 2016

Hot little girl in high school[1]

I'm a very compassionate person (with a very high IQ)[2]
Just think, in a couple of years I'll be dating you[3]
It must be a pretty picture, you dropping to your knees[4]
Come here, I'll show you how life works.[5] Please[6]

1 Key Capitol Hill hearings, 30 December 2015
2 *The Rachel Maddow Show*, CNBC, 26 May 2017
3 Campaign speech in Des Moines, Iowa, 11 December 2015

Get the oil, get the oil, get the oil[1]

You heard me, I would take the oil[2]
I know, it's crude[3]

1 Appearance in an advert for Trump Steaks, 2007
2 Referring to a dinner at Mar-a-Lago with President Xi Jinping of China during interview, *Mornings with Maria*, Fox Business, 12 April 2017
3 Tweet promoting the meatloaf at Mar-a-Lago, 29 December 2011
4 Tweet promoting the Donald J. Trump signature clothing line at Macy's, 26 June 2014
5 *The O'Reilly Factor*, Fox News, 28 April 2016
6 Statement, White House website, 20 January 2017
7 Trump's first address to Congress, 28 February 2017
8 Tweet, 15 April 2014
9 Referring to his plans for North Korea in an interview with Maria Bartiromo, Fox Business, 12 April 2017
10 Tweet promoting Trump International Toronto, 2 November 2012
11 Tweet congratulating Andre Reed, 29 July 2014

Treat yourself to the very, very best life has to offer[1]

The most beautiful piece of chocolate cake[2]

The world's greatest steaks[1]

The best meatloaf in America[3]

The best ties & shirts at the best prices[4]

Beautiful humvees and rifles[5]

A state-of-the-art missile defense system[6]

The fantastic new F-35 fighter jet[7] – exclusively available at Macy's[8]

An armada, very powerful[9]

Luxury at its finest[10]

You deserve it![11]

1 *Access Hollywood* tape, 2005
2 Proclaiming National Sexual Assault Awareness and Prevention Month, 31 March 2017

You can do anything[1]

At the heart of our country is the emphatic belief that every person has unique and infinite value[2]

(I just start kissing them)[1]

On average there are more than 300,000 instances of rape or other sexual assault that afflict our neighbors and loved ones every year[2]

(It's like a magnet)[1]

We all share the responsibility to reduce and ultimately end sexual violence[2]

(I don't even wait)[1]

Recent research has demonstrated the effectiveness of changing social norms that accept or allow indifference to sexual violence[2]

(You can do anything)[1]

Our families, schools, and communities must encourage respect for women[2]

(Grab them by the pussy)[1]

Together, we can and must protect our loved ones, families, campuses, and communities from the devastating and pervasive effects of sexual assault[2]

(You can do anything)[1]

1 Tweet criticising Megyn Kelly for interviewing Ted Cruz, 17 March 2016
2 Tweet criticising Megyn Kelly, 27 January 2016
3 Interview with Don Lemon on CNN, referring to Megyn Kelly's questioning of him during the US Republican Presidential primaries, 7 August 2015
4 Tweet criticising Megyn Kelly, 16 February 2016

Crazy Megyn Kelly:[1] a Haiku

Lightweight reporter[2]
Blood coming out of her wherever[3]
Get a life Megyn[4]

1 Tweet referring to Anthony Weiner, 25 April 2013
2 Tweet, children spelt wrongly in tweet, 8 October 2012
3 Tweet referencing Newtown child killings, 17 December 2012
4 *Washington Times* interview about Trump's guns, an H&K .45 and a .38 Smith & Wesson, 14 November 2012
5 Campaign rally at Sioux Center, Iowa, 24 January 2016
6 Describing how he would have stopped a would-be attacker at an Ohio campaign rally, 12 March 2016
7 Tweet referencing the murder of Jessica Ridgeway, 13 October 2012
8, 9 Tweet, 19 November 2012

Pervert alert[1]

Got to do something about these missing chidlren grabbed by the perverts[2]

#Angels[3]

I own a couple of different guns[4]

I could stand in the middle of 5th Avenue and shoot somebody[5]

Boom, boom, boom[6]

Death to the pervert killer[7]

It makes me feel so good to hit "sleazebags" back[8]

Much better than seeing a psychiatrist (which I never have!)[9]

1, 2 Donald Trump (1997), *Trump: The Art of the Comeback*, Times Books: New York
3 *Playboy* interview, 2004
4 Presidential bid announcement at Trump Tower, 16 June 2015

Women have one of the great acts of all time[1]

The smart ones act very feminine and needy, but inside they are real killers[2]

I wouldn't mind if there were an anti-Viagra[3]

That's the kind of thinking our country needs right now[4]

1 Tweet criticising Rosie O'Donnell, 15 December 2011
2 TV clip used in Hillary Clinton attack advert, 23 September 2016
3 *Entertainment Tonight*, CBS, 2006
4 Tweet criticising Rosie O'Donnell, 9 November 2012

Sad sack Rosie:[1] a Haiku

That fat, ugly face[2]
She talks like a truck driver[3]
She's got no talent[4]

1, 2, 3 'Thank you' rally in Wisconsin, 13 December 2016
4 Tweet, 25 December 2013

No days off[1]

We are going to say "Merry Christmas" again[2]

Merry Christmas[3]

O.K., Christmas is over, now we can all go back to the wars
of life[4]

1 Speech in Hilton Head, South Carolina, 30 December 2015
2 Rally in New Hampshire, 17 September 2015
3 Interview with *The Washington Post*, 5 January 2016
4 *CNN Newsroom*, CNN, 9 August 2016
5 Campaign rally in Fresno, California, 27 May 2016
6 Press conference, 26 May 2016
7 Tweet criticising mainstream media outlets, 11 January 2017

There's something going on that we don't know about[1]

A lot of people are saying that bad things are happening out there[2]

A lot of people are talking about it[3]

I'm not saying that, and I'm not a conspiracy person[4]

I'm not going to say it, because I'm not allowed to say it, because I want to be politically correct[5]

I know nothing about it[6]

The people truly get what's going on[7]

1 *Wall Street Journal*, 24 January 2016
2 Impromptu call to NBC News, 24 November 2015
3 Inaugural Address, 20 January 2017

Photographic memory[1]

I have the world's greatest memory[2]

The forgotten men and women of our country will be forgotten no longer[3]

1 Interview with Chris Wallace, *Fox News Sunday*, Fox News, 18 October 2015
2 Speech in Hilton Head referencing the dangers of global warming, Hilton Head, South Carolina, 30 December 2015
3 Remarks regarding his concerns about global warming at the Republican Jewish Coalition, 7 December 2015
4 Letter co-signed by Trump and family to Barack Obama, urging him to coordinate global action on climate change, 6 December 2009
5 Tweet, 10 September 2013
6 Complaining that the room was too hot at a campaign town hall event in Virginia, 26 July 2016

We'll be fine with the environment[1]

They say Don't use hair spray, it's bad for the ozone;[2]
Global warming is our biggest threat;[3]
If we fail to act now, it is scientifically irrefutable that there
will be catastrophic and irreversible consequences for
humanity and our planet.[4]
Too boring![5]
Try turning on the air conditioning[6]

1 Tweet, 25 November 2014
2, 3, 4 *The New York Times* interview, 29 March 2009
5 Alabama pep rally, *CNN Tonight*, CNN, 21 August 2015
6 Fox News *Special Report*, 6 October 2015
7 Tweet, 29 June 2013
8 Interview with Wolf Blitzer, CNN, 21 March 2016
9 In reference to his German roots in the documentary *Kings of Kallstadt*, dir Simone Wendel, 2014
10 Presidential bid announcement at Trump Tower, 16 June 2015
11 Tweet, 28 September 2014
12 Campaign rally in Muscatine, Iowa, 25 January 2016

Good genes[1]

"All men are created equal"[2]
Well it's not true[3]
Some are smart, some aren't[4]

Do we believe in the gene thing? I mean, I do![5]
I'm blessed with good genes[6]
Good (great) brain.[7] Good-sized hands.[8] German blood.[9]

We have people that are stupid[10]
They cannot help the fact that they were born
fucked up[11]
Slow horses don't produce fast horses[12]

1 Tweet criticising John McCain, 11 October 2016
2 Tweet criticising John McCain, 16 July 2015
3 Tweet criticising John McCain, 9 February 2017
4 Forum in Ames, Iowa, 18 July 2015

Very foul-mouthed Sen. John McCain:[1] a Haiku

Graduated last[2]
Doesn't know how to win[3]
Not a war hero[4]

1 Tweet about the *Celebrity Apprentice* final, 20 May 2011
2 Tweet, 5 September 2014
3 Said to President Xi Jinping of China over chocolate cake, as referenced on *Mornings with Maria,* 12 April 2017
4 Tweet, 25 March 2013

Get ready for some excitement[1]

China is going to complete 59 new theme parks by 2020[2]
We've just fired 59 missiles[3]
Fireworks![4]

1 Tweet criticising Megyn Kelly, 10 August 2015
2 Campaign rally in Hilton Head, South Carolina, 30 December 2015
3 Oval Office interview with Associated Press, 23 April 2017
4 'Politics and Eggs' event, Manchester, New Hampshire, November 2015
5 Response to a question in a Reddit 'Ask me anything', 27 July 2016
6 Tweet, 4 February 2015

I am the innocent (pure) one![1]

I love the universe[2]
The bigness of it all[3]
Space is terrific[4]
Honestly I think NASA is wonderful[5]
Reach out, seek and explore[6]

1 Tweet criticising Jeb Bush's Republican Presidential nominee campaign, 23 March 2016
2 Tweet criticising Jeb Bush's Republican Presidential nominee campaign, 2 January 2016
3 Republican debate in South Carolina, 14 February 2016
4 Tweet criticising Jeb Bush's Republican Presidential nominee campaign, 17 February 2016

Low energy Jeb:[1] a Haiku

Low energy "stiff"[2]
Said he would take his pants off[3]
He wants to look cool[4]

1 Outlining his approach to foreign policy in speech in Walterboro, South Carolina, 17 February 2016
2 Speech at the National Federation of Republican Assemblies Convention in Nashville, Tennessee, 29 August 2015
3 Tweet referring to Jeb Bush's slogan 'Jeb can fix it', 1 November 2015
4, 5 Report on interview with CNN's Jake Tapper, 19 June 2015
6 Rally in Las Vegas, 8 October 2015
7 Key Capitol Hill hearings, CSPAN, 9 October 2015
8 Statement on Facebook following release of *Access Hollywood* tapes, 7 October 2016

I want to be good[1]

I really want to be a nice person and I am a nice person[2]

I never thought of Jeb as a crook[3]
I actually felt bad because I hit him very hard one day . . .
and I said, why am I hitting him so hard?[4]
I think he's a wonderful man[5]

I called Rubio a lightweight[6]
He may be a nice guy. I really don't know him[7]

I've said and done things I regret[8]

1 Meeting with the *Washington Post* editorial board, 21 March 2016
2 Interview with Wolf Blitzer, CNN, 21 March 2016
3 Tweet promoting (and quoting from) his book *The Midas Touch*, 6 April 2012

My hands are normal hands[1]

I buy a slightly smaller than large glove[2]

The five fingers represent the five key factors every entrepreneur dreaming of success must master[3]

1, 5 Paris Climate Accord exit speech, 1 June 2017
2 Tweet, 17 September 2012
3 Tweet, 19 October 2015
4 Tweet, 25 January 2014
6 Tweet, 27 May 2013

Pittsburgh, not Paris[1]

Kate Middleton is great – but she shouldn't be sunbathing in the nude[2]

It's really cold outside[3]

NBC News just called it the Great Freeze[4]

Thus, as of today, the United States will cease all implementation of the non-binding Paris Accord[5]

We want global warming right now![6]

1 Interview with Tucker Carlson, Fox News, 17 March 2017
2 Letter to *The New York Times*, 11 September 2005
3, 4 *Fox Friends* interview, Fox News, 28 February 2017
5 Tweet, 18 November 2014

I love to read[1]

I've read John Updike, I've read Orhan Pamuk, I've read
Philip Roth[2]
I believe a lot of the stories are pure fiction[3]
They just pull it out of the air[4]
Gang of liars[5]

1 Tweet criticising Bill Maher, 29 January 2014
2 Tweet criticising Bill Maher, 31 October 2013
3 Tweet regarding Maher's failure to pay $5 million to charity if Trump could prove he was not 'the spawn of his mother having sex with an orangutan', 4 February 2013
4 Tweet referring to the GOP nomination, 4 October 2015

Failing comedian Bill Maher:[1]
a Haiku

A very dumb guy[2]
So today I will sue him[3]
I'm going to win![4]

1 Campaign rally in Hilton Head, South Carolina, 30 December 2015
2 White House press conference, 16 February 2017
3 South Carolina Campaign rally, 10 February 2016
4 Tweet, 20 August 2016
5 Tweet criticising Barack Obama, 5 May 2014
6 Tweet criticising Democratic Party healthcare policies, 26 April 2017
7 Tweet, 20 February 2013
8 Tweet criticising Barack Obama, 23 September 2014
9 Tweet criticising Chinese government, 6 September 2012
10 Tweet promoting Trump National Golf Club, 18 March 2015
11 Tweet, 16 April 2016
12 Tweet criticising Hillary Clinton, 3 August 2016
13 Tweet, 13 April 2013
14 Tweet criticising bailouts paid to banks, 10 February 2012
15 Tweet criticising Obama administration's foreign policy, 7 March 2017
16 Tweet supporting Miami-Dade Mayor Carlos Giménez's dropping of county sanctuary policy, 26 January 2017
17 Tweet responding to Breitbart polling of US Presidential candidate support, 28 July 2016
18 Tweet criticising Obama administration's taxation policies, 3 July 2012
19 Tweet, 22 May 2014
20 Tweet criticising perceived Chinese foreign and economic policies, 2 January 2017
21 Tweet praising Russian foreign policy efforts, 10 September 2013
22 Tweet, 25 April 2015
23 Speech after winning the Florida, Illinois and North Carolina primaries, 15 March 2016

I have the best words[1]

I think I'll say a few words[2]

Okay. Are you ready?[3]

Good![4] Bad![5] Sad![6] Loser![7] Terrible![8] Outrageous![9] Spectacular![10]
Fantastic![11] Scandal![12] Smart![13] Stupid![14] Weak![15] Strong![16]
Great![17] Shameful![18] Beautiful![19] Nice![20] Dangerous![21]

Love those words[22]

And there's so many more![23]

1 Oval Office interview with Reuters, 24 February 2017
2 Tweet promoting Trump Hotel Panama, 21 November 2013
3 News conference at Trump Tower, 11 January 2017
4 Speech after winning the Florida, Illinois and North Carolina primaries, 15 March 2016
5 Referring to judging beauty pageant, *The Howard Stern Show*, 2005
6 Describing the scene in Studio 54, *Playboy* interview, 2004
7 Speech in Hilton Head, South Carolina, 30 December 2015
8 *Access Hollywood* tape, 2005
9 Tweet about how handsome Stephen Baldwin's mother allegedly thinks Trump is, 24 March 2013
10 Tweet referring to Jeb Bush's photoshopped image in a campaign advert, 22 August 2015
11 Describing Russian politician Alexander Lebed, *The New Yorker*, 19 May 1997
12 Used in speech in Manchester, New Hampshire, 28 October 2016
13 Tweet responding to Republican Presidential nominee polling data from Idaho, 7 March 2016
14 Used in tweet criticising Barack Obama, 12 March 2012

A dream[1]

Trump Panama offers fine dining, five pools and luxury rooms[2]
In those rooms you have cameras in the strangest places[3]
I'm watching . . . we have televisions all over[4]
You see these incredible-looking women[5]
The top models in the world getting screwed on tables[6]
Then, all of the sudden, the cameras swerve[7]
And all of a sudden I see her[8]
Stephen Baldwin's mother[9]
She's totally changed her look[8]
She's now got the big phoney tits[8]
A black left hand and much different looking body[10]
That nose is a piece of rubber[11]
And she says:[12]
I love your potatoes.[13]

Weird[14]

1, 7 Graduation speech to coastguard cadets, 17 May 2017
2 Tweet, 10 December 2015
3 Speech in Des Moines, Iowa, 11 December 2015
4 Tweet, 30 May 2016
5 White House town hall with CEOs and business leaders, CSPAN, 4 April 2017
6 Tweet, 27 February 2016

Look at the way I've been treated lately[1]

I should have been Time Magazine's Person of the Year[2]

Just like I should have gotten the Emmy for The Apprentice[3]

I should have easily won the Trump University case[4]

I should have won New York state but I didn't[5]

I unfairly get audited by the I.R.S. almost every
single year[6]

No politician in history – and I say this with great surety –
has been treated worse or more unfairly[7]

1   Speech in Novi, Michigan, 30 September 2016
2   *The Apprentice*, season 1 episode 1
3   *The Apprentice*, season 2 episode 1
4   *The Apprentice*, season 3 episode 1
5   *The Apprentice*, season 4 episode 1
6   *The Apprentice*, season 5 episode 1
7   *The Apprentice*, season 6 episode 1
8   *The Apprentice*, season 7 episode 1
9   *The Apprentice*, season 8 episode 1
10 *The Apprentice*, season 9 episode 1
11 *The Apprentice*, season 10 episode 1
12 *The Apprentice*, season 11 episode 1
13 *The Apprentice*, season 12 episode 1
14 *The Apprentice*, season 13 episode 1
15 *The Apprentice*, season 14 episode 1
16 Letter firing FBI Director James Comey, 9 May 2017

My two favorite words[1]

You're fired[2]
You're fired[3]
You're fired[4]
You're fired[5]
You're fired[6]
You're fired[7]
You're fired[8]
You're fired[9]
You're fired[10]
You're fired[11]
You're fired[12]
You're fired[13]
You're fired[14]
You're fired[15]
You are hereby terminated[16]

1 Victory speech in New Hampshire, 9 February 2016
2 Presidential bid announcement at Trump Tower, 16 June 2015
3 Referring to Syrian refugees at a campaign rally in Newton, Iowa, 11 November 2016
4, 5 Tweet, 29 March 2016. It was a pen.
6 First solo White House press conference, 16 February 2017
7 Tweet, 10 March 2013
8 Campaign rally in Mount Pleasant, South Carolina, Key Capitol Hill hearings, 8 December 2015
9 *Playboy* interview, March 1990

What's going on? What's going on?[1]

Does my family like me?[2]

Where are the women?[3]

Why is this reporter touching me as I leave news conference?[4]

What is in her hand?[5]

I don't know which microphones to hold[6]

My hair – should I change it?[7]

I'm sort of like, what am I doing?[8]

I don't want to be President. I'm 100% sure[9]

1 Press conference, 16 February 2017
2 Tweet criticising representatives of Victoria's Secrets' treatment of Kate Upton, 4 February 2013
3 Tweet criticising opposition to offensive drawings of Prophet Muhammad, 4 May 2015
4 Speech in Fresno, California complaining about wildlife protection rules, 27 May 2016
5 *Face the Nation*, CBS, 6 December 2015
6 Tweet about birds killed by wind turbines, 12 October 2012
7 Deleted tweet, 31 May 2017
8 Tweet promoting the Donald J. Trump clothing line at Macy's, 13 December 2013
9 Tweet referencing trial of Oscar Pistorius, 21 October 2014
10 Victory rally in Orlando, Florida (referring to the electoral map), 16 December 2016
11 On being fact-checked about his claim over electoral college victory, BuzzFeed, 14 February 2014

I don't know[1]

Victoria's Secret reps[2]
Horrible and mocking cartoons of Jesus[3]
A certain kind of three-inch fish[4]
The guy with the dirty hat[5]
"Wing bangers"[6]
Covfefe[7]
Really beautiful suits and cufflinks[8]
Cold blooded murder[9]
(Bloody, so red, so red, it's beautiful)[10]
Who knows what's in the deepest part of my mind?[11]

You have to be everything[1]

I can be a killer and a nice guy[2]
I can be very military. High rank![3]
I can be more presidential than anybody[4]
You gotta say, I cover the gamut[5]
I am pro-life[6]
I'm a people person[7]
I'm a king[8]
I am a champion[9]
I'm also very much of a germaphobe[10]
I'm a counterpuncher[11]
I'm President, and you're not[12]
I'm a person that very strongly believes in academics[13]
I am a defender of Miley Cyrus[14]
(Miley, don't let them get you down)[15]
I am a handwriting analyst[16]
I'm the world's greatest writer of 140 character sentences[17]
I am your voice[18]
I am what I am[19]

1 Donald Trump (1987), *The Art of the Deal*, Random House: New York
2 Tweet, 29 December 2014
3 Press conference with Muhammadu Buhari of Nigeria, 30 April 2018 (the correct name for the aircraft is Super Tucano)
4 Remarks to marines at Quantico, 15 December 2017
5 Tweet, 25 April 2018, in response to Kanye West's tweet of the same date, proclaiming Trump as his 'brother'.
6 Remarks at Make America Great Again rally in Pennsylvania, 10 March 2018

Art of the deal[1]

I like making deals – preferably big deals[2]

For example, we recently sold Nigeria 12 US A-29 Super Cutano aircraft[3]

They gave me this hat. It says: "Presidential Helicopter Squadron".[4] Very cool![5]

I mean, that's worth a ten-minute meeting, right?[6]

1 Trump referring to the button he presses to order a Diet Coke, in an interview with the *Financial Times*, 26 April 2017
2 Tweet in response to Kim Jong-un's statement that his nuclear button is always on his desk, 2 January 2018
3 Republican nomination acceptance speech, 21 July 2016
4 Remarks at a National Republican Congressional Committee Dinner, 21 March 2017
5 Rally in Hilton Head, South Carolina, 30 December 2015
6 Quoted in the *New Yorker*, 19 May 1997
7 Tweet in reply to Arsenio Hall, 23 August 2012
8 Tweet, 21 August 2015

Everyone does get a little nervous when I press that button[1]

I too have a nuclear button[2]
My greatest source of pride and joy[3]
It is a much bigger and more powerful one than his[2]
Constructed with American steel[4]
And my button works![2]
No, sir.[5] You wouldn't want to play nuclear weapons with this fucker[6]
(Just joking.[7] I would never condone violence.[8])

1 Speech at campaign rally for Luther Strange in Huntsville, Alabama, 22 September 2017
2 Tweet referring to Kim Jong-un, 12 April 2013
3 Tweet referring to Kim Jong-un, 26 April 2013
4 Interview with *Bloomberg News*, 1 May 2017

Little "Rocket Man":[1] a Haiku

North Korean man child[2]
28-year-old wack job[3]
I would absolutely meet with him[4]

1 Address to March for Life participants in Washington, 19 January 2018

2 Press conference in Singapore after North Korea summit with Kim Jong-un, 12 June 2018

3a, b & c Interview with *Fox and Friends*, 15 June 2018 (3a in reference to Kim Jong-un; 3b in reference to Xi Jinping; 3c in reference to Melania Trump on his birthday)

4 Interview on *60 Minutes*, 14 October 2018

5 Speech at Make America Great Again rally at Great Falls, Montana, referring to Russia, China and 'other countries', 5 July 2018

6 Remark at 2018 White House Business Session, in response to the Prime Minister of India in a trade deal, 26 February 2018

The gift of friendship[1]

He is very talented[2]

He speaks and his people sit up at attention. I want my people to do the same[3a]

We had a tremendous 24 hours[2]

We hugged. We kissed[3b]

(I got a lot of good kisses.)[3c]

We fell in love[4]

Adversaries can indeed become friends[2]

I didn't know that[4]

Getting along is really a nice thing[5]

Huh[6]

1 Reportedly said at an Oval Office meeting about DACA immigration deal, 11 January 2018
2 Tweet denying saying anything derogatory about Haiti, 20 January 2018
3 Tweet about the need for a wall between America and Mexico, 18 January 2018
4 Tweet referring to MS-13 gang members, 23 February 2018
5 Tweet regarding refugees in America, 12 February 2017
6 Referring to Namibia, but spoken as 'Nambia' during address to a lunch meeting of African leaders, 20 September 2017
7 Presidential Determination on Major Drug Transit or Major Illicit Drug Producing Countries for Fiscal Year 2018, issued 13 September 2017
8 Tweet about Ebola patients, 31 July 2014
9 Lunch meeting with members of Congress, 27 June 2018
10 Speech at No Labels convention, New Hampshire, 12 October 2015
11 Speech in Janesville, Wisconsin, 29 March 2016

Shithole countries[1]

Haiti[2], Mexico[3], El Salvador[4]

Libya[5], Nambia[6], Ecuador[7]

Why are we having all these people from shithole countries come here?[1]

All have AIDS[1]

KEEP THEM OUT OF HERE![8]

...

Okay?[9] It's always good to compromise[10]

All of the ladies can come, but the guys can't[11]

1 Tweet about Obama, 26 March 2014
2 Tweet, 7 October 2013
3 Tweet about Charles Krauthammer, 9 July 2015
4 Tweet in reference to his proposal of a wall between the United States and Mexico, 1 April 2018

How totally stupid is this guy?[1]

"We build too many walls and not enough bridges."
– Isaac Newton[2]

What a dope![3] NEED WALL![4]

1 Tweet regarding illegal immigration, 22 June 2018
2 Speech on immigration in Phoenix, Arizona, 31 August 2016
3 Remarks at a Customs and Border Protection roundtable,
  2 February 2018
4 Remarks at a roundtable on immigration with regards to
  California, 16 May 2018
5 Interview with *Fox News*, referring to his order of four thousand
  television sets, 18 October 2015
6 Weekly address, referring to the NASA Transition Authorization
  Act, 25 March 2017
7 Appearance on *The Howard Stern Show*, referring to
  Afghanistan, 16 July 2008
8 South Carolina rally for the GOP primaries, 25 June 2018
9 *The Apprentice Star Wars* promo, 2006
10 Speech to Conservative Political Action Conference at Oxon
  Hill, Maryland, 24 February 2017
11 Campaign speech in Raleigh, North Carolina, 5 July 2016
12 GOP convention speech in Cleveland, Ohio, 21 July 2016
13 Tweet in support of Ed Gillespie, 7 November 2017
14 Referring to the proposed border wall, speech at Pensacola Bay
  Center, Pensacola, Florida, 9 September 2016

Aliens[1]

There are at least 2 million criminal aliens now inside the country[2]

They're pouring in[3]

These aren't people[4]

You know where they come from?[5]

Outer space[6]

A breeding ground for terrorists[7]

So, we're going to create a Space Force and it's going to be great[8]

It's the Trump Death Star[9]

The biggest, the best, absolutely the most technologically sophisticated battlestation ever, in the entire galaxy[9]

Nobody will dare question our military might again[10]

Heads will spin[11]

Illegal border crossings will go down[12]

Crime will be gone[13]

And Mexico will pay for it[14]

138

I don't think Angelina Jolie is good looking:[1] a Haiku

A solid seven[2]
Bad skin.[1] Her lips are too big[2]
I'm just not a fan[1]

Very big negotiations[1]

I've never met a good negotiator that tells you he's a good negotiator[2]

.

.

.

.

I'm a good negotiator[3]

1 Proclaiming June as National Ocean Month, 31 May 2017
2 Comments referring to ISIS, said during a speech in Iowa, 13 November 2015
3 Tweet, 4 July 2013

The mighty oceans[1]

I would bomb the shit out of them[2]
Sorry folks, I'm just not a fan of sharks[3]

1 Tweet, 18 April 2018
2 Tweet referring to Senator Mark Warner and Robert Muller, 25 June 2018
3 Appearance on *Imus in the Morning*, referring to his friends, 1 December 2005
4 Interview with *Playboy*, referring to discussions over a possible luxury hotel in Moscow, March 1990
5 Referring to a member of the Wake Forest NCAA at the White House Sports and Fitness Day, 30 May 2018
6 Referring to pundits in speech at Oklahoma City, Oklahoma, 25 September 2015
7 Referring to CNN in interview with *Fox and Friends*, 26 April 2018
8 Referring to the Robert Mueller investigation at a White House press conference, 15 June 2018
9 Press conference before Air Force One departure, 4 May 2018
10 Speech on the National Security strategy, 18 December 2017
11 Appearance on *Imus in the Morning* in the middle of campaign rallies, 26 August 2015
12 Remarks at the National Thanksgiving Turkey Pardoning Ceremony, 21 November 2017
13 Tweet, claiming sole responsibility for LiAngelo Ball's release from jail, after Ball was arrested for shoplifting in China, 22 November 2017

NO COLLUSION
(except by the Dems)![1]

13 Angry Democrats on a Witch Hunt[2]

Three of them are major alcoholics[3]

Seven are Russian[4]

One of them is 6'11[5]

Most of them are morons okay?[6]

Every one of them is against me[7]

Everybody has got massive conflicts[8]

That's not a fair situation[9]

However . . .[10]

In the end it doesn't matter[11]

Today, in the spirit of Thanksgiving, I will grant a Presidential pardon to a turkey[12]

ME[13]

1 Tweet, 18 April 2018
2 Tweet referring to James Comey, 13 April 2018
3 Tweet referring to James Comey, 27 April 2018
4 Tweet referring to James Comey, 11 June 2017

Slippery James Comey, the worst FBI director in history:[1] a Haiku

Untruthful slime ball[2]
He lied all over the place[3]
Very "cowardly!"[4]

1 Speech at Conservative Political Action Conference, 23 February 2018
2 Sung at his Inaugural Prayer Ceremony, 20 January 2017
3 Medal of honour presentation ceremony, 24 May 2018
4 Tweet regarding taking a knee during the National Anthem, 24 September 2017
5 During speech at the Susan B. Anthony Campaign for Life gala, 22 May 2018
6 Referring to the state of the White House, in speech at Easter Egg Roll event at the White House, 2 April 2018
7 Making an aside to Steve Mnuchin during speech at a Foxconn facility in Wisconsin, 28 June 2018
8 Asking Kellyanne Conway to stand, during address to Working Group of Mayors, 24 January 2018
9 Asking Vice President Mike Pence to stand at the Governors' Ball, 26 February 2017
10 Asking Ivanka Trump to stand up, during speech at the White House on the six-month anniversary of the tax cuts legislation, 29 June 2018
11 Referring to the national anthem at the Super Bowl, during speech on tax reform in Cincinatti, Ohio, 5 February 2018
12 Speech to the NRA leadership forum in Dallas, Texas, 4 May 2018
13 Comment during speech on the Infrastructure Initiative, Richfield, Ohio, 30 March 2018
14 Asking Melania Trump to stand up during speech at a charity dinner in New York, 20 October 2016

A nightmare[1]

Oh, say! can you see . . .[2]
Please stand up. Please.[3]
. . . by the dawn's early light . . .[2]
Standing with locked arms is good, kneeling is not acceptable[4]
. . . What so proudly we hailed . . .[2]
Steve, stand. You have no problems standing[5]
. . . at the twilight's last gleaming . . .[2]
This guy is in better shape than all of us.[5] We call it sometimes tippy-top shape.[6] Right, Steve?[7]
. . . Whose broad stripes and bright stars . . .[2]
Stand up, Kellyanne.[8] Mike, just stand up for a second[9]
. . . through the perilous fight . . .[2]
Stand up Ivanka. Stand up, honey[10]
. . . O'er the ramparts we watched . . .[2]
Everybody stood up yesterday[11]
. . . were so gallantly streaming . . .[2]
We all proudly stand for the national anthem.[12] We love our great American flag, don't we?[13] Stand up Melania![14] Stand up![10]

1 Comment during Republican Party convention, 21 July 2016
2 Speech at White House Christmas tree lighting ceremony,
   1 December 2017
3 Comment at meeting of the Senate Finance Committee,
   27 November 2017
4 Tweet, 8 May 2013
5 Comment during White House press conference about a
   Veterans Fundraiser 31 May 2016
6 Tweet, 19 December 2012
7 Tweet referring to an upcoming interview with Bret Baier,
   9 April 2015

The Christmas of Trump[1]

The Christmas Story begins 2,000 years ago with a mother, a
father, their baby son and the most extraordinary gift of all:[2]

A tremendous tax cut[3]

I'm giving away money![4]

One other thing that's important to know[5]

I'll open the Miss Universe Pageant as Santa tonight[6]

6:00 P.M. on Fox. Don't miss it![7]

1 Appearance in Macy's commercial, 2012
2 Appearance in Macy's commercial, 2008
3 Tweet in response to a Twitter user's suggestion that he did not understand a question, 30 April 2013
4 Repeating shouted comment about Ted Cruz by audience member at New Hampshire rally, 8 February 2016
5 Tweet describing Kim Jong-un, 11 November 2017
6 Tweet describing Kim Jong-un 11 November 2017
7 Tweet describing Jeb Bush, 21 January 2016
8 Tweet referring to Anthony Weiner, 25 April 2013

What's with the get-up, Kringle?[1]

How dreary would be the world if there were no
Santa Claus?[2]
Sarcasm, dummy.[3] He's a pussy[4]
He lives in a fantasy[5]
Short and fat.[6] Sad sack[7]
Parents, make sure your children have him blocked[8]

1 Praising Brett Kavanaugh at rally in Southaven, Mississippi, 2 October 2018
2 Praising Brett Kavanaugh at mentioned at rally in Montoursville, Pennsylvania, 20 May 2019
3 Praising Brett Kavanaugh at rally in Charleston, West Virginia, 21 August 2018
4 Praising Brett Kavanaugh at rally in Springfield, Missouri, 21 September 2018
5, 6 Rally in Belgrade, Montana, 3 November 2018

Perfect human being[1]
Brett Kavanaugh:[2] a Haiku

Great, brilliant man.[3]
Fantastic man.[4] Nothing in
your past.[5] You're perfect[6]

1 Accomplishments, misspelled by Trump in handwritten note seen at Rose Garden Press Conference, 23 May 2019
2 Speech at Department of Health and Human Services, 25 October 2018
3 Tweet, 12 January 2019
4 Tweet, 18 April 2018
5 Address to Future Farmers of America in Indianapolis, 27 October 2018
6 Speech in Portland, Maine, 3 March 2016
7 Interview on The Howard Stern Show, 11 January 1993
8 Welcoming the 2018 NCAA FCS college national football champions, North Dakota, 4 March 2019
9 GOP Fundraiser in Fargo, North Dakota, 7 September 2018
10 Tweet, 5 May 2019

Achomlishments[1]

A few examples:[2]

I fired Lyin' James Comey[3] (worst FBI director in history)[4]

I've had many meetings with farmers in my office[5] (ruined my carpet)[6]

I was actually faithful to my wife[7] (nothing is impossible)[8]

The list goes on[9]

Most successful first two years of any President in history[10]

Acknowledgements

A million thank-yous to Paula Amaral, Frankie Leong and Danny Kwong; to the Trump Twitter Archive, the Trump Archive and the American Presidency Project; to Gordon Wise and Niall Harman at Curtis Brown; to Hannah Knowles, Rona Williamson, Leila Cruickshank, Vicki Rutherford and everyone else at Canongate; and to Belinda Sears, John Sears, Tom Sears, Claire Chesser and Grace McGeoch.